D1315139

Cats

Are Night Animals

LINDENHURST MEMORIAL LIBRARY
LINDENHURST, NEW YORK 11757

by Joanne Mattern

Reading consultant: Susan Nations, M.Ed., author/literacy coach/consultant in literacy development
Science and curriculum consultant: Debra Voege, M.A., science and math curriculum resource teacher

Please visit our web site at: www.garethstevens.com
For a free color catalog describing Weekly Reader® Early Learning Library's list
of high-quality books, call 1-877-445-5824 (USA) or 1-800-387-3178 (Canada).
Weekly Reader® Early Learning Library's fax: (414) 336-0164.

Library of Congress Cataloging-in-Publication Data

Mattern, Joanne, 1963-
  Cats are night animals / by Joanne Mattern.
    p. cm. — (Night animals)
  Includes bibliographical references and index.
  ISBN-13: 978-0-8368-7846-2 (lib. bdg.)
  ISBN-13: 978-0-8368-7853-0 (softcover)
  1. Felidae—Juvenile literature. I. Title.
  QL737.C23M278   2006
  599.75—dc22   2006030882

This edition first published in 2007 by
Weekly Reader® Early Learning Library
A Member of the WRC Media Family of Companies
330 West Olive Street, Suite 100
Milwaukee, Wisconsin 53212 USA

Copyright © 2007 by Weekly Reader® Early Learning Library

Editor: Tea Benduhn
Art direction: Tammy West
Cover design and page layout: Scott M. Krall
Picture research: Diane Laska-Swanke

Picture credits: Cover, title page © Kim Taylor/naturepl.com; p. 5 © Joel Sartore/National Geographic
Image Collection; p. 7 © Carine Schrurs/naturepl.com; p. 9 © Anup Shah/naturepl.com; p. 11 © Novastock/
Photo Researchers, Inc.; p. 13 © Aflo/naturepl.com; p. 15 © Jane Burton/naturepl.com; p. 17 Scott M. Krall/
© Weekly Reader Early Learning Library; p. 19 © Jason Edwards/National Geographic Image Collection;
p. 21 © Beverly Joubert/National Geographic Image Collection

All rights reserved. No part of this book may be reproduced, stored in a retrieval system,
or transmitted in any form or by any means, electronic, mechanical, photocopying, recording,
or otherwise, without the prior written permission of the copyright holder.

Printed in the United States of America

1 2 3 4 5 6 7 8 9 10 10 09 08 07 06

Note to Educators and Parents

Reading is such an exciting adventure for young children! They are beginning to integrate their oral language skills with written language. To encourage children along the path to early literacy, books must be colorful, engaging, and interesting; they should invite the young reader to explore both the print and the pictures.

The *Night Animals* series is designed to help children read about creatures that are active during the night. Each book explains what a different night animal does during the day, how it finds food, and how it adapts to its nocturnal life.

Each book is specially designed to support the young reader in the reading process. The familiar topics are appealing to young children and invite them to read — and reread — again and again. The full-color photographs and enhanced text further support the student during the reading process.

In addition to serving as wonderful picture books in schools, libraries, homes, and other places where children learn to love reading, these books are specifically intended to be read within an instructional guided reading group. This small group setting allows beginning readers to work with a fluent adult model as they make meaning from the text. After children develop fluency with the text and content, the books can be read independently. Children and adults alike will find these books supportive, engaging, and fun!

— Susan Nations, M.Ed., author/literacy coach/
consultant in literacy development

Two spots of light shine in the darkness. What are they? They are the eyes of a cat!

There are many kinds of cats. Lions, tigers, and bobcats are all wild cats. Most wild cats sleep a lot during the day. They are more active at night.

Wild cats **hunt** in the dark. The animals they hunt are also active at night. Some wild cats hunt small animals, such as rabbits. Others hunt big animals, such as deer.

Pet cats are like wild cats in many ways. They are night animals, too. They eat and play during the day, but they also sleep a lot.

At night, pet cats like to hunt. Some chase mice. Others **stalk** their favorite toys.

All cats see well at night. The centers of a cat's eyes open wide to let in light.

The light **reflects**, or bounces, off of special **cells**. The reflected light helps a cat see and makes its eyes shine in the dark.

a cat's eye

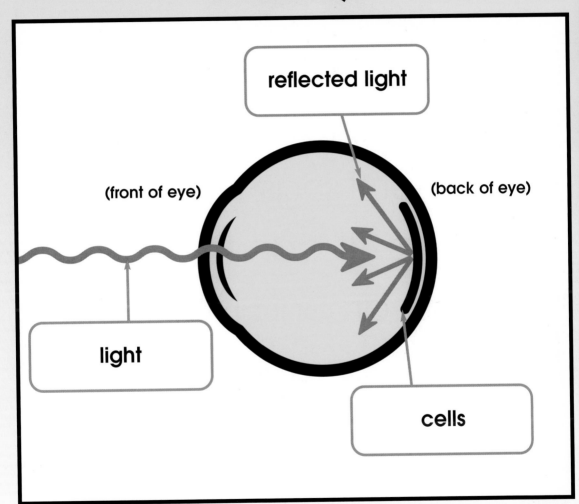

reflected light

(front of eye)

(back of eye)

light

cells

A cat's **whiskers** help it at night, too. A cat can feel things with its whiskers. It can feel objects around it to know when something is in its path.

whiskers

Wild or tame, all cats are **expert** night animals.

Glossary

cells — the smallest parts of the body

expert — the best or very good at doing something

hunt — to find and kill other animals for food

reflects — sends back light from an object so the object looks like it is shining

stalk — to crouch down and move toward an object very quietly and slowly

whiskers — long, stiff hairs on a cat's face that help it feel its way around in the dark

For More Information

Books

American Shorthair Cats. Nancy Furstinger (Checkerboard Books)

Cats. Usborne Beginners (series). Anna Milbourne (Usborne Books)

Cougars. Animals That Live in the Mountains (series). JoAnn Early Macken (Gareth Stevens)

Tiger. Busy Baby Animals (series). Jinny Johnson (Gareth Stevens)

Web Site

For Kids . . . About Cats
kids.cfa.org
This site has cat games and fun facts about different cat breeds and colors. It also gives you the inside scoop on cat shows.

Publisher's note to educators and parents: Our editors have carefully reviewed this Web site to ensure that it is suitable for children. Many Web sites change frequently, however, and we cannot guarantee that a site's future contents will continue to meet our high standards of quality and educational value. Be advised that children should be closely supervised whenever they access the Internet.

Index

About the Author

Joanne Mattern has written more than 150 books for children. She has written about unusual animals, sports, history, world cities, and many other topics. Joanne also works in her local library. She lives in New York State with her husband, three daughters, and assorted pets. She enjoys animals, music, reading, going to baseball games, and visiting schools to talk about her books.